AMAZING ADVENTURE PUZZLE THRILLERS

THE MAD SCIENTIST'S SECRET

MARVIN MILLER

Illustrated by Tony Tallarico

SCHOLASTIC INC.
New York Toronto London Auckland Sydney

Also by MARVIN MILLER

YOU BE THE JURY
YOU BE THE JURY: COURTROOM II
YOU BE THE JURY: COURTROOM III
YOU BE THE JURY: COURTROOM IV
YOU BE THE DETECTIVE
YOU BE THE DETECTIVE II
WHO DUNNIT?

For Matty

ISBN 0-590-49438-4

Copyright © 1994 by Marvin Miller.
All rights reserved. Published by Scholastic Inc.

12 11 10 9 8 7 6 5 4 3 2 1   4 5 6 7 8 9/9

Printed in the U.S.A.   40

First Scholastic printing, January 1994

Contents

I
Going Undercover

You are sitting in the headquarters of the Tip Top Secret Service. It is assigned special secret missions that are too difficult for the regular Top Secret Service.

"Why did you send for me?" you ask.

Tip Top Secret Agent Horner tugs at his bow tie and fastens you with a steely stare.

"We have been given one of the most important missions ever handed to us," he says. "This assignment requires someone whom no one would ever suspect. Someone with brains . . . and courage."

Horner looks you squarely in the eyes. "Someone like you."

Horner leans back in his chair. "But you must give me your word that no one will know you are working for us."

He suddenly slaps both hands on the desk. "I mean NO ONE!"

Startled, you nod in agreement.

Horner leans forward and whispers softly. "Even your name will be a secret," he says.

1

He hands you a card. "Here. This is your secret identification. It is your code name. Use it whenever you want to identify yourself to one of our agents."

You stare at the card with a puzzled look. "But what does it say?" you ask. "It looks like a crossword puzzle."

WHAT IS YOUR SECRET CODE NAME?

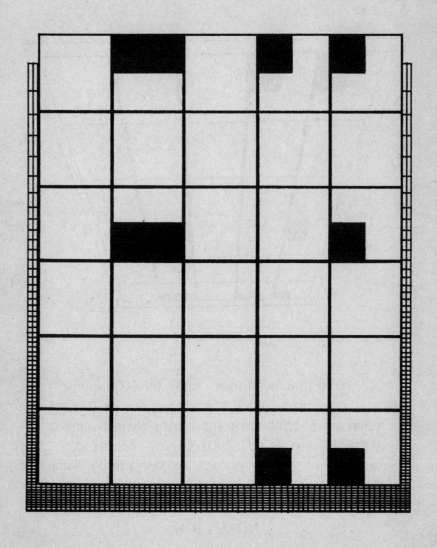

SOLUTION

Hold the bottom of the page near the tip of your nose. Then close one eye.

Tilt the page away from you so that your eye is almost level with the bottom edge of the page. Then read the letters at a steep slant.

Suddenly your code name pops out. ACE!

II
Your Assignment

"**L**isten to me carefully, ACE," Agent Horner says. "We have just learned of a criminal mastermind named Dr. XXX. His plan is to smuggle a chemical called SLUDGE into school cafeterias.

"Once anyone eighteen or younger gets a taste of SLUDGE, they turn into ZOMBIES who will obey any order given by Dr. XXX.

"Dr. XXX plans to have every kid in the country under his command."

"But how can he do this?" you ask.

Horner continues his explanation.

"The SLUDGE tastes just like school cafeteria food. Dr. XXX has thousands of spies to help him. Posing as cafeteria workers, they'll add SLUDGE to the school lunches. The kids will turn into ZOMBIES without ever suspecting a thing.

"There's only one chance to stop Dr. XXX. There's an antidote called MUCK that deactivates SLUDGE. Just one drop of it can make SLUDGE harmless."

Horner slowly presses his fingers together. He

stares directly at you, his face stiffening as he speaks.

"We want you to find the MUCK and pour it into the SLUDGE."

You watch in silence while Agent Horner takes off his bow tie and chews the edge for a moment. "You have a very difficult assignment, ACE. The fate of the entire world could be in your hands, so this EMERGENCY KIT has been prepared for you," he says as he rips open a polka-dotted backpack and pours the contents on his desk.

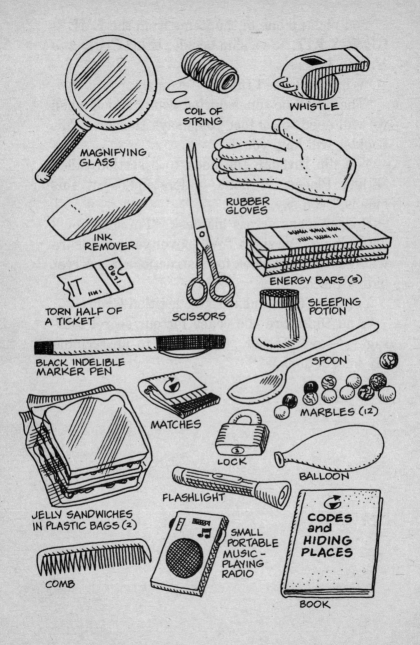

MAGNIFYING GLASS

COIL OF STRING

WHISTLE

RUBBER GLOVES

INK REMOVER

ENERGY BARS (3)

TORN HALF OF A TICKET

SCISSORS

SLEEPING POTION

BLACK INDELIBLE MARKER PEN

SPOON

MATCHES

MARBLES (12)

LOCK

BALLOON

JELLY SANDWICHES IN PLASTIC BAGS (2)

FLASHLIGHT

CODES and HIDING PLACES

COMB

SMALL PORTABLE MUSIC-PLAYING RADIO

BOOK

You pick up one of the items from the EMER-GENCY KIT. It's a slim booklet titled *Codes and Hiding Places*.

"What do I need this for?" you ask.

"There will be times during your mission when we will need to contact you," says Horner. "This booklet will help you."

You flip through the book to a section called Hiding Places. "I don't understand what this means," you say.

Horner leans across his desk. "I'm sure you'll figure it out," he sighs. "Whenever you are unsure where to go next, look for instructions in a secret hiding place."

You turn to the next section, titled Codes.

"And those are the codes for our secret messages," says Horner. "Use them to unscramble my instructions."

CODES

CONFUSION CODE

ONLY WRITE DOWN THE LETTERS IN PARENTHESIS. THEN SPACE THE LETTERS TO FORM WORDS.

EXAMPLE:

$$CODE = (H) \div (OWA) \times 6 - (RE)$$
$$(YO) < {}^N_K > (U?)$$

MESSAGE = *HOW ARE YOU?*

SCRAMBLE CODE

BREAK UP THE LETTERS INTO PAIRS. THEN REVERSE THE TWO LETTERS IN EACH PAIR. LASTLY, SPACE THE REVERSE PAIRS TO FORM WORDS. DROP THE LETTER **X**.

EXAMPLE:

CODE = HTNI FKS AXT.

MESSAGE = *THINK FAST*

The book still seems puzzling, but you decide you'll wait until you need it to figure it out. You put everything from the EMERGENCY KIT back in the polka-dotted backpack.

"Where do I start?" you ask, trying to hide your nervousness.

Horner pulls a jelly donut from his pocket and munches as he explains.

"The first part of your mission is to locate Jonathan Nutt. He is a scientist who works for Dr. XXX. He has manufactured a small amount of the antidote MUCK."

He finishes the jelly donut and pulls another from his pocket. You begin to wonder how many donuts he's got in there.

"We have been told that Jonathan Nutt goes to the Greenville post office every Monday afternoon at three o'clock to pick up an envelope from Dr. XXX. Each envelope contains a large sum of money in payment for his work."

Agent Horner waves a third jelly donut in the air as he speaks.

"Find Nutt, and follow him. Oh . . . and there's one more thing. You also must destroy the written formula for SLUDGE so it can never be used again. It's written in permanent ink that's almost impossible to erase. That's why we put a special ink remover in your EMERGENCY KIT."

"But why can't I just tear up the paper it's written on?" you ask.

"That's the problem," replies Horner. "It's tattooed on something."

"Tattooed?" You're a little afraid to hear what comes next. "On what?"

Horner taps the donut on the desk as he answers.

"It's tattooed on the head of Dr. XXX's pet ape." He takes a bite of the donut. "Dr. XXX shaved its head, wrote down the formula for safe keeping, and then let the ape's hair grow back."

"You mean . . ." you say, unable to finish your sentence.

Horner nods as he chews the jelly donut. "Now you have your complete mission. First, find Jonathan Nutt and the antidote MUCK. Then find the SLUDGE and deactivate it by pouring the MUCK into it. Then you must erase the formula tattooed on the head of the ape! Good-bye, and good luck!"

You turn to make your way out of the office. As you near the door, Agent Horner calls out, "Do you want a jelly donut?"

You're eager to get started on your mission, so you pretend not to hear.

"Oh, one more thing!" Agent Horner calls after you. "The first agent we sent on this mission had a rough time. Agent Cody was turned into . . . a ZOMBIE!!!"

III
The Chase Begins

When you enter the Greenville post office, the wall clock shows nearly 3:00 PM. Just in time. Jonathan Nutt must be picking up his mail.

Four people are lined up at the service window. Jonathan Nutt is the third person in line.

He is wearing a wig, but you recognize him by the small scar on his right cheek.

What do you do now? Maybe Agent Horner has a plan for you.

You pull out *Codes and Hiding Places* and open it to the first page:

Hiding Place #1
A FACE BUT NO MOUTH
NO FINGERS BUT IT POINTS
NO FEET BUT IT RUNS

WHERE IS THE HIDING PLACE?

SOLUTION

The hiding place is the clock on the post office wall. The front of the clock is its *face*, the hands *point* to the time, and it's always *running*!

You stare up at the clock hanging on the post office wall. Where is Horner's secret message?

Your eyes slowly circle the clock's border. All of a sudden you notice a tiny piece of paper sticking out behind it, wedged between the clock and the wall. Your hunch was right.

You stand on your toes and reach. It's just beyond your grasp. Then you jump up, snatching the piece between your fingers. Down comes the folded paper.

Opening it, you stare at a confusing jumble of letters. It must be written in code.

OGVO REO THT PES OMTS
AETAR DNDINE ITYF OYR UES
FLSA HK MIOH IWE SVLS
IOTA D?Y
   LEIVW SLIFLL OOL JWN OTAA
HNATUXT.

TURN BACK TO YOUR CODE BOOK AND DECIDE WHICH CODE TO USE. WHAT IS THE SECRET MESSAGE?

SOLUTION

The coded message reads:

GO OVER TO THE POSTMASTER AND IDENTIFY YOURSELF. ASK HIM "HOW IS ELVIS TODAY?"
ELVIS WILL FOLLOW JONATHAN NUTT.

IV
How Is Elvis Today?

Yₒᵤ read the message twice, not knowing exactly what it means. Just who is Elvis, anyway?

Then you glance around the lobby and see that Nutt is standing at the service window.

A man in a post office uniform walks over to you and smiles warmly. "It's closing time," he says. "If you want to buy stamps, you'd better hurry over to the window."

Above the pocket of his shirt is a badge. POST-MASTER is printed on it. It's the person Agent Horner wants you to contact!

You hesitate and then blurt out your instructions. "I'm Ace. How is Elvis today?"

The man looks around. "Follow me," he whispers. Together you head toward the back room.

Inside, he reaches under his desk and lifts out a bird cage, then sets it on top of the desk.

"This is Elvis."

You stand there completely surprised. The postmaster takes a white bird from the cage and cradles it in his arm. A tiny camera is tied around its neck.

The postmaster continues. "Wait outside with Elvis. When Jonathan Nutt leaves, set Elvis free. He will follow Nutt.

"The camera is set to take an aerial picture. After five minutes, Elvis will fly right back to you.

"Then open the rear of the camera and you will find an instantly developed photo. It will show you where Nutt went."

The postmaster holds out Elvis. Grasping the bird gently, you tuck it inside your shirt.

As you leave, you hear the postmaster's voice. "Good luck, Ace!"

You stand outside the post office, waiting for Nutt to leave. You don't have to wait long. Soon he runs through the post office door and hurries toward the main street.

As he passes, you toss Elvis into the air. The bird spreads its wings and flies off after Nutt. Both disappear into the distance.

You wait again.

How many minutes have passed? You can't be sure. It seems like Elvis has been gone a very long time. Five minutes. Maybe ten.

You're beginning to get very nervous, when suddenly you spot a white speck that seems to grow larger. It's a white bird flying directly toward you. It's Elvis!

The bird swoops down and glides into your open arms.

A rush of excitement sweeps over you as you

quickly open the back of the small camera. Inside is a tiny photo.

You take the magnifying glass out of your EMERGENCY KIT. There's Nutt! He's at the pier!

Running at top speed, you follow Nutt's trail. But when you get to the pier there is no sign of Jonathan Nutt — only a lone fisherman.

You dash toward him, catching your breath as you speak. "Have you seen anyone just get here?"

The man yawns. "I guess I fell asleep. I haven't seen a single fish, much less a person."

Nutt must have arrived while the fisherman was napping. But where did he go?

You look across the lake and notice an island in the distance.

"What's that over there?" you ask the fisherman, pointing toward the horizon.

The man takes off his hat and runs his fingers through his hair. "Oh, you mean Fireball Island? That used to be a place where people had summer homes. But no one lives there anymore."

Of course! A deserted island would be a perfect hideout for a fiendish scientist.

A small rowboat is tied up beside the pier. "Is this yours?" you ask the fisherman.

"Nope," he answers with a shrug. "It belongs to the game warden."

"Thanks," you reply as you jump in and untie its rope. "Tell the game warden not to worry,

I'll return the boat," you shout as you row away.

You row up to the sandy beach of Fireball Island and tie the boat to a wooden post.

A line of tall trees forms a giant wall beyond the beach. They seem to serve as a silent warning to stay away.

Suddenly you see a path, half hidden by overgrown foliage. It must lead into the island.

Pushing aside overgrown leaves, you trudge along the path until you come to a clearing. Up ahead are four cottages.

They look abandoned. The fisherman was right, you think. No one must live here anymore.

But something seems very strange. Suddenly you realize that one of the cottages isn't empty. Someone is inside.

WHICH ONE IS IT?

SOLUTION

The spiderweb covering the door of one of the cottages is broken. Someone must have recently entered that cottage.

V
Up in the Air

Slowly you sneak up to the cottage. You tiptoe next to a window and try to peek inside. But it is completely covered over by a heavy curtain.

What do you do now? You don't want Nutt to find you.

Boldly you march up to the front door. Maybe you can slip inside.

You carefully turn the doorknob, but it stops after a quarter turn. The door must be locked.

You step back off the front step. Then you circle the cottage, peeking into each window. All have curtains, hiding whatever might be behind them.

You move to the rear of the house and look up at a window on the second floor. It's partly open.

You notice a vine hanging down from the roof and running right alongside the open window. The end dangles not far below it.

That's it! If you can reach the end of the vine, you can climb up and into the window.

You stand on your toes, trying to grab the vine. But it's no use. The dangling end is at least two feet beyond your reach.

Is there something you can stand on? You look all around, but there is nothing in sight. Not a box. Not a barrel. Nothing.

Then you get an idea. Sure! That will do it.

HOW DO YOU REACH THE VINE?

SOLUTION

You take the shovel and start digging a hole. You pile each shovel of dirt one on top of the other until you have made a huge mound.

VI
The Secret Laboratory

You climb the mound of dirt until you reach the top. Standing on your tiptoes, you grab for the end of the dangling vine. You can now reach it!

Slowly you pull yourself up, hand over hand, until you hang by the open window. The room inside is dark. Silently you pull yourself onto the ledge and slide through the open window into the room.

Everything around you looks like junk. Old furniture is piled all over. You see a large trunk. And there are piles and piles of old magazines. This must be a storage room.

A beam of light in the corner catches your eye. You tiptoe over. The light is coming from a hole in the floor. It's shining up from the room below.

You drop to your knees and look down the hole. There he is! It's Jonathan Nutt, sound asleep on a big cushiony sofa.

You scan the room as far as you can see. Directly below the hole is a wooden table. Bottles full of chemicals stand on top of it.

You've discovered Jonathan Nutt's laboratory!

The place he makes MUCK, the antidote to SLUDGE.

In the center of the table is a half-empty bottle. Maybe, just maybe, it contains the antidote you are looking for.

If only you can get the antidote while Nutt is still asleep. But how?

You poke your arm through the hole and try to reach the flask. But your arm is much too short.

Then you look around the storage room. In a corner is a hollow metal pole, resting against the wall. Maybe you can use it to lift out the MUCK. But how?

Then you have an idea. Your EMERGENCY KIT. Maybe something in it can help.

You quickly zip open the kit and search inside. Suddenly you have your solution.

WHAT CAN YOU USE TO LIFT UP THE
BOTTLE OF MUCK?

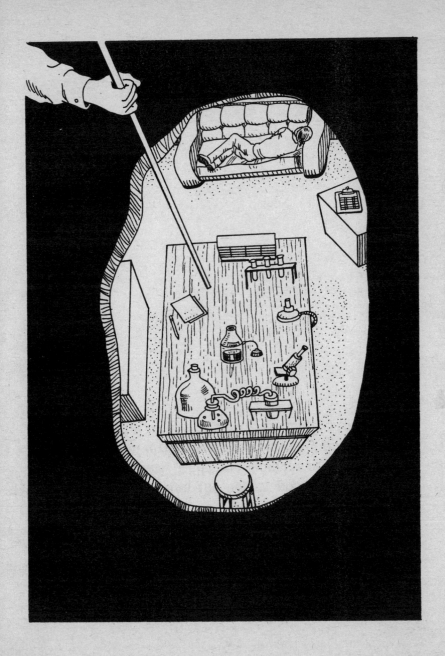

SOLUTION

You take the balloon from the emergency kit and slip it over an end of the hollow pole.

Then you lower it down the hole and into the bottle.

Blowing through the hollow pole, you expand the balloon until it fills up the inside of the bottle.

After you form a seal, you carefully pull up the pole inch by inch. The bottle is clinging to it!

VII
The Antidote

There! You've done it. You hold up the bottle and read the word on the label. It says MUCK!

You stare at it hopefully. In your hands is the secret to deactivate SLUDGE. It is your only hope to rescue the country from Dr. XXX and his fiendish plan.

You quickly snap the cap on the bottle and slip it into your EMERGENCY KIT.

Just then, the door to the room swings open.

There, inside the doorway, stands Jonathan Nutt! He must have come up a back stairway while you were working.

Nutt is wearing an angry scowl.

"You know too much for your own good," he says with a snarl. "There's only one way to deal with the likes of you."

Nutt grabs some rope and a gray metal box. Then he shoves you out the door.

Once outside, Nutt marches you across the high grass to a small shack. He kicks open the door.

Nutt turns on the light. Rows of giant fish tanks

31

are lined up against the walls. Fish of every kind are swimming inside them.

"This is my experimental biology room," boasts Nutt. "I use the venom from these fish to make the poison that Dr. XXX uses."

He pushes you into a wooden chair.

"You're lucky Dr. XXX has all the SLUDGE, or I'd turn you into a ZOMBIE," he says with a nasty snarl. "But don't worry. I've got something else in store for *you!*"

Nutt ties you tightly to the chair.

You try to move. But you can't.

Nutt opens the metal box. Your heart sinks as you watch him carefully lift out six red sticks. It's dynamite!

Nutt puts the explosives on the floor next to the fish tank.

Your eyes widen as he strikes a match. Then he bends down and lights the fuse.

"There!" barks Nutt. "This room has served its purpose. I have no use for it anymore. In five minutes the fuse will reach the dynamite. And KABOOM!! Both you and the fish will be blown to pieces. You'll be a seafood salad!"

Nutt's insane laughter echoes in your ears as he heads out the door.

HOW CAN YOU ESCAPE?

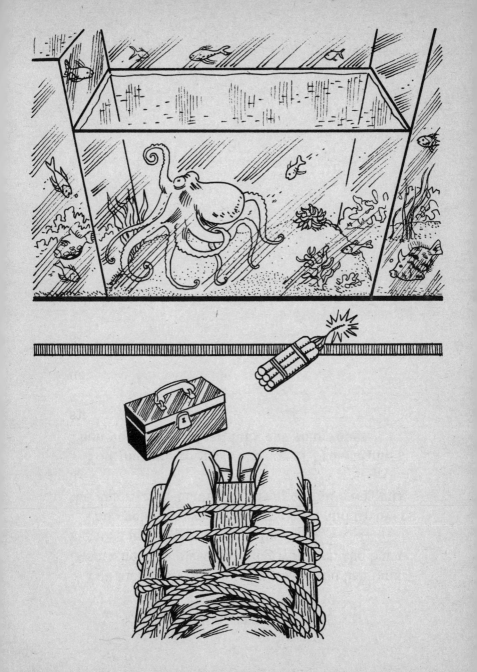

SOLUTION

You kick the gray box directly at the fish tank. It smashes the glass, pouring water on the burning fuse and dousing the flame.

Then you inch yourself to the tank and tip over the chair. Still bound tightly, you fall over with it.

You manage to grab a piece of broken glass. Then you use it to carefully cut your ropes.

VIII
Escape!

You pull off the ropes wrapped around you and kick open the cabin door. The coast is clear.

Swiftly you run, ducking behind trees to avoid being seen by Nutt.

When you reach the beach, you look around in bewilderment. The boat that you came in is gone!

You switch direction and run toward a steep hill up ahead.

When you reach the top, your eyes gaze across a flat grassy plain. You stop to catch your breath. At the far end of the plain you see a cliff.

You run toward it. Standing near the edge, you look straight down below.

There! A boat is anchored in the water. But how can you reach it?

You stare in bewilderment at the dozens of steps that lead down from the cliff.

They may be your route to escape.

HOW DO YOU REACH THE BOAT?

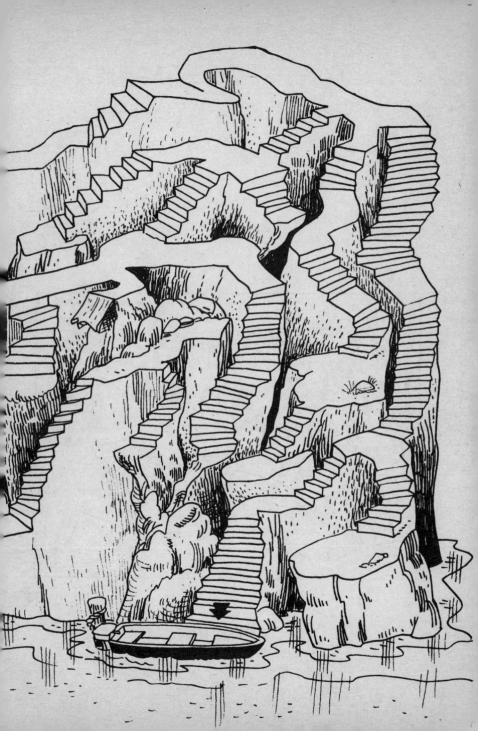

SOLUTION

IX
Back on Track

Jumping in the boat, you weigh anchor. At last you are on your way! In the distance you spy a coastline. It looks like a safe destination.

You stretch out on the deck to relax your aching bones. After a half hour of smooth sailing, the boat safely reaches the shore. You breathe a sigh of relief.

About 100 yards up ahead is a small house. Feeling very tired from your narrow escape, you step out of the boat and trudge toward it.

You knock on the door.

No answer.

You try knocking again.

Nothing.

Slowly, you turn the knob and enter. The smell of musty air whiffs past you.

Looking all around, you see that no one is there. What do you do next?

A wood plaque above the doorway catches your eye. On it is an emblem that looks familiar.

You pull out *Codes and Hiding Places*. It has an emblem on the cover. The one above the door matches it exactly. You must be inside a meeting house of the Tip Top Secret Service!

Maybe Horner hid your instructions in this room. But where? You flip open the book and turn to the next page.

HIDING PLACE #2
SMILE AND IT IS GLAD
FROWN AND IT IS SAD

You know that the answer to the riddle will reveal the location of your instructions.

WHERE IS THE SECRET HIDING PLACE?

SOLUTION

The hiding place is the mirror.
When you look into it with a smile, your reflection is glad. When you frown, it looks sad.

You walk over to the mirror. It is streaked all over with dusty smudges.

The mirror is fairly large with a fancy frame. You look around the edges to see if a message is wedged between the frame and the wall, like the message you found behind the clock at the post office.

But there is no message.

Then your hand searches around the frame for a secret message carved into its surface. But you feel nothing unusual.

Maybe the message is hidden behind the mirror.

You carefully lift the mirror off the wall and turn it around. It's much heavier than it looks. You wouldn't want to drop it and break it. You're not superstitious, but you have heard some people say that breaking a mirror means seven years of bad luck will follow.

Gently, you rest one edge of the frame on the floor. Then you look at the back of the mirror.

No luck. Nothing is on the other side, either.

Perhaps there's some trick to the mirror. Is it a two-way mirror?

You wave your hand back and forth behind the mirror, but you can't see through the mirror. You wave your hand back and forth on the other side, but it still doesn't work.

The mirror is just an ordinary mirror.

Frustrated, you rehang the mirror on the wall. As you do, you glance at your dusty reflection.

Your hair is a mess, but you feel a lot better than you look. The narrow escape from Nutt's marine biology room hasn't worn you down.

As you take a step back, a beam of sunlight strikes the mirror at an angle. There seem to be strange-looking scratch marks inside the streaks.

Could this be a code? Maybe it is the message you have been looking for.

TURN BACK TO YOUR CODE BOOK AND DECIDE WHICH CODE TO USE. WHAT IS THE SECRET MESSAGE?

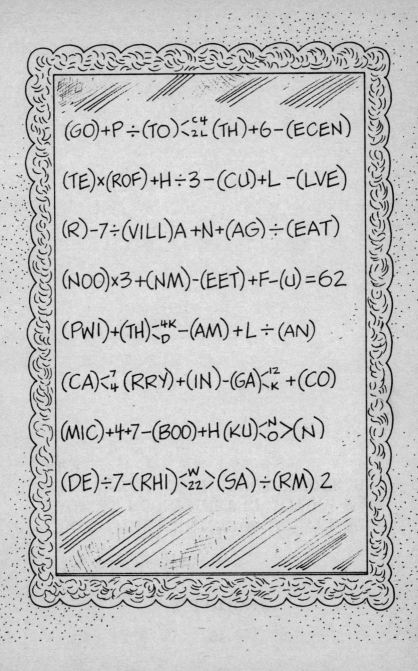

$(GO)+P \div (TO) <^{C4}_{2L} (TH)+6-(ECEN)$

$(TE) \times (ROF)+H \div 3-(CU)+L-(LVE)$

$(R)-7 \div (VILL)A+N+(AG) \div (EAT)$

$(NOO) \times 3+(NM)-(EET)+F-(U)=62$

$(PWI)+(TH) <^{4K}_{D} -(AM)+L \div (AN)$

$(CA) <^{7}_{4} (RRY)+(IN)-(GA) <^{12}_{K} +(CO)$

$(MIC)+4+7-(BOO)+H(KU) <^{N}_{O} > (N)$

$(DE) \div 7-(RHI) <^{W}_{22} > (SA) \div (RM)\,2$

SOLUTION

The coded message reads:

GO TO THE CENTER OF CULVER VIL-
LAGE AT NOON. MEET UP WITH A MAN
CARRYING A COMIC BOOK UNDER HIS
ARM.

X
Which Way?

You read the message a second time. The man with the comic book must be your contact agent.

You rush out the door. The sun blazes down overhead. It must be close to noon. There's no time to waste.

In the distance is a road. Maybe it leads to Culver Village.

After you've been on the road a few minutes, you see something headed toward you. It's a woman on a white horse. You motion for her to stop.

The lady reins in the horse.

"Howdie," she says, "I'm Rhonda Pratt. My farm is just up the road a bit."

She looks down at you, a little concerned. "You look kinda lost. Whereabouts are you headed?"

"Is this the way to Culver Village?" you ask.

Rhonda breaks into a broad smile. "Yup!" she nods. "Right now you are in Kilmer Landing. But keep going. Culver Village is about ten minutes up the road.

"Just follow the sign when you come to a fork in the road."

"Thanks," you reply as you dash away.

Rhonda Pratt was right. After a few minutes you reach a fork. Three roads branch off in different directions.

But which road should you take? And where is the signpost?

You look down at a grassy patch where the roads intersect. There, lying on the ground, is the signpost. Someone must have knocked it from its hole.

You kneel down to read the words printed on the arrows. One says CULVER VILLAGE. But in which direction is it pointing?

It is almost noon. If you take the wrong road you will be too late to meet your contact with the comic book.

Then you get an idea. After studying the arrows again, you hurry down one of the roads.

WHICH ROAD DO YOU FOLLOW?

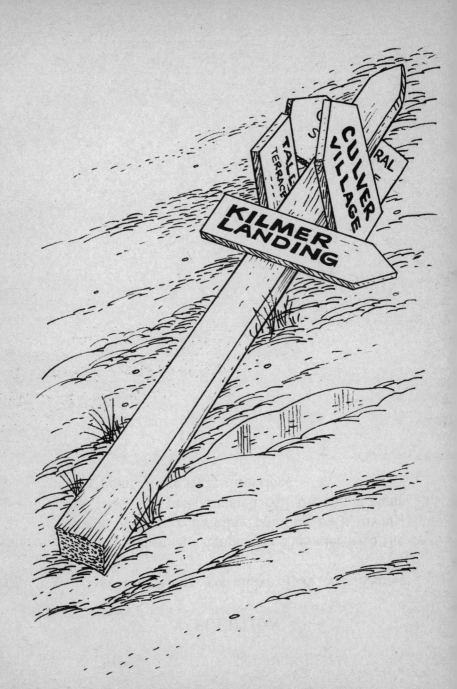

SOLUTION

You remember you have just left Kilmer Landing.

You replace the signpost in the hole, with the arrow of Kilmer Landing pointing back toward the road you just traveled. All the other signs now point in the right directions.

XI
The Agent with the Comic Book

The main street of Culver Village is lined with quaint shops.

People are milling everywhere. You see a flower shop, a book shop, and more.

You spot a boy in a striped shirt blowing bubble gum. A boy in a football uniform is crossing the street. You see several women carrying packages, but only one of them is wearing a skirt with polka-dots and stripes. A man walks out of a shop. He is carrying a small tree.

A large banner stretches from one side of the street to the other.

The banner reads CULVER VILLAGE ANNIVERSARY CELEBRATION.

That explains why the street is so crowded. But how will you find the agent with the comic book? He might be anywhere in the busy crowd.

WHERE IN THE CROWD IS YOUR CONTACT?

SOLUTION

The agent with the comic book is looking in the
window of the candy shop.

XII
Contact

You wind your way through the crowd and head for the candy shop. You stop next to the man with the comic book and stare at the store window.

Now what? What should you say?

Then you remember. Maybe you should use your code name.

You move closer to the man and pretend to admire a large glass jar filled with jelly beans.

"I'm Ace," you whisper, glancing at him out of the corner of your eye.

The man holding the comic book smiles and extends his hand. "Glad to have you aboard, Ace." He shakes your hand with a firm grip.

"My name is Bolt," he says. "I hear you've been following Nutt. Did you find the antidote?"

You pat your polka-dotted EMERGENCY KIT. "It's in here," you say. "Safe and sound."

"The spies that work for Dr. XXX are having a big meeting in the Crumb Building," says Bolt. "They're planning to spread out across the country after Dr. XXX sends them the SLUDGE. We have to find out the details."

Bolt points to a cluster of buildings in the distance. "The Crumb Building is the tall one," he says.

As you walk toward your destination, a flashing sign on the roof next to the Crumb Building catches your eye. The sign says HOTEL POLK.

You walk into the Crumb Building. Beyond the lobby is a corridor. It leads to two large oak doors at the other end.

"Dr. XXX's spies are meeting in the room behind those doors," says Bolt. "We've got to see what's in there, but we've got to be careful."

He points at the black-and-white tiled floor of the corridor. "This floor is wired to detect outsiders. The only way to reach the room is to walk on the right tiles. Otherwise, an alarm will go off."

"What do you mean?" you ask Bolt.

Your partner continues. "To get to the room without setting off the alarm, we have to walk on a white tile, then a black tile, and so on. We have to switch from white to black to reach the doors. That way we bypass the alarm."

Bolt frowns. "But I'm not sure how." Then he pauses and looks down at you. "Want to go first?"

START ON A WHITE TILE AND MOVE TO A BLACK ONE. HOW DO YOU REACH THE DOORS WITHOUT SETTING OFF THE ALARM? YOU MAY NOT STEP DIAGONALLY.

SOLUTION

58

XIII
Lock Up

You've done it! Standing silently near the oak doors, you motion for Bolt to follow.

But Bolt misses the last black tile. He steps on a white one instead. Alarms go off everywhere!

The two of you break into a run, heading back to the entrance. But it's too late. The oak doors swing open and out rush four spies.

One tackles Bolt.

Another one grabs you by the shoulders.

The spies push you and Bolt against the wall.

"What are you two doing here?" they ask.

You and your partner remain silent.

"You both know too much for your own good," says one of the spies. "We're locking you upstairs until we can figure out what to do with you."

Two spies shove you and Bolt into an elevator. One presses the twelfth-floor button.

When the elevator opens, they lead you both out. While one spy watches, the other opens the door to a room. They push you inside.

You hear the door lock with a click.

A voice in the hall shouts, "We're posting a guard. Don't try anything tricky."

The room is completely dark.

"Are you okay, Bolt?" you ask.

A voice answers weakly. "My head feels like a sledgehammer hit it. But I think I'll be all right. Search around for a light switch."

Your hand gropes the wall near the door. You find the switch and flip it on.

The room has a long table in the center and a chair at each end. A shabby-looking carpet covers the floor.

"What do we do now?" you ask.

Bolt puts a finger to his lips. "Shh," he says in a low voice. "This room is bugged with a hidden microphone."

He points at the ceiling light. A tiny black object is stuck to it. You can barely see it.

"They put us here so they can listen in," whispers your partner. "That way they can find out what we're up to."

You and Bolt must plan a way to escape. But how can you plan? Dr. XXX's spies can hear your every word, even the slightest whisper.

Then you get an idea.

You zip open your EMERGENCY KIT.

HOW CAN YOU PREVENT THE SPIES
FROM HEARING YOU?

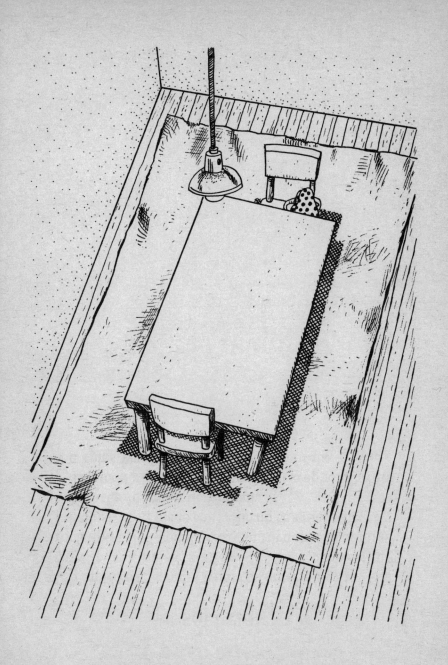

SOLUTION

You take the radio from the emergency kit and turn it to a music station. "I love that old-time rock and roll," you say as you turn up the volume full blast. You place the radio on the table directly below the hidden microphone.

The loud music blares into the microphone. Now the spies won't be able to hear you talk.

XIV
Trapped

The music from the radio blasts all around the room. It's so loud you can hardly hear yourself think. But you don't mind — this is one of your favorite songs.

Bolt tiptoes to a corner of the room and motions for you to join him.

"Here is my plan," he whispers in your ear. "Let's make them think we've discovered a vent in the ceiling and we're going to escape through it.

"I'll stand behind the door. When the guard comes into the room to stop us, I'll jump him."

Bolt looks to see if you understand. You give him a nod.

"Let's go," you say, switching off the radio.

In a loud voice, Bolt pretends to speak to you. "Look up there at the ceiling vent. It looks big enough for us to crawl through."

"Wow! It sure does," you answer loudly. "If we stand on a chair, I'll bet we can reach it. Boy, are those spies dum-dums."

Bolt sneaks behind the door. You silently wait for the guard to make his move.

Seconds later, the door flies open. A burly spy, with a club in his hand, rushes in.

Bolt steps out from behind the door and silently steps up behind the guard. He sticks out his first three fingers, bends them slightly, then lightly taps the guard on the back of the neck. The guard collapses to the floor.

"How did you do that?" you ask.

"Oh, it's just a little-known self-defense secret I learned when I was a student in Brazil," says Bolt. "It comes in handy from time to time."

You step over the unconscious guard. He's sleeping like a baby.

"Follow me," whispers Bolt. You both race into the hall toward an exit door.

But then you trip and land spread-eagled on the floor. Slightly dazed, you pick yourself up, just in time to see the exit door close behind Bolt. You run over and turn the knob.

The exit door is locked!

Bolt calls from the other side of the door. "It's no use. The exit door won't open. It must be jammed. I'll use the stairs and you take the elevator. Hurry before the others arrive. I'll meet you outside."

You run to the elevator and press the button, but nothing happens. You press the button again.

Still nothing.

Then the truth hits you. The elevator has been turned off.

Then you see a piece of newspaper underneath the exit door. Inch by inch, the newspaper slides into view. Someone on the other side of the door is pushing it into the hall.

Suddenly you see it burst into flames. One of the spies has set it on fire!

The flames from the paper leap higher and higher. The spies are trying to burn you out!

You hurry over to the flaming paper and stomp on it, trying to put out the flames. It's no use. The fire has ignited the hallway carpet. The flames leap higher as smoke begins to fill the hallway.

You look around. There, at the end of the hallway, is a fire hose. You grab it and turn on the water full blast, trying to douse the flames. The fire hose is doing its job.

You keep the hose aimed at the flames. But suddenly the hose starts to sputter. The stream of water has turned into a dribble. Someone must have turned off the main water supply! The flames begin to leap up once again.

The heat and the smoke are unbearable. You know you won't be able to survive in the hallway for long.

You back up toward the end of the hall as the flames of the burning carpet creep toward you. How can you escape?

You open the rear window and look down. Below you is the next building, the Hotel Polk. If only you could jump out the window and onto the hotel's roof.

But it's too far to jump. You don't think you can make it. Flames from the burning carpet creep closer and closer, backing you against the window.

HOW CAN YOU ESCAPE ONTO THE ROOF OF THE HOTEL POLK?

SOLUTION

You toss one end of the fire hose out the window. It tumbles down to the roof of the Hotel Polk. Then you carefully climb down the hose.

XV
Signaling For Help

The end of the fire hose dangles about three feet from the hotel roof. You easily jump, landing on your feet.

From the hotel roof you look out over the town. The sun is setting on the horizon.

Now all you need to do is get into the hotel and escape. You notice a door in one corner of the roof. It must lead inside the hotel. Escape should be easy.

But when you pull the door handle, it won't budge. It is sealed as tight as a drum. You pull harder, but without any luck. The door must be locked from the inside.

You walk to the edge of the roof and stare at the street below. Bolt must be down there somewhere.

Then suddenly you see him hiding behind a telephone pole.

You cup your hand to your mouth and yell, "Bolt!" But your voice fades into the night air.

"Bolt!" you shout, as loudly as you can. Still no answer. Bolt doesn't move. He can't hear you.

Maybe you can attract your partner's attention. Suppose you throw something at him. No. It won't work. He is too far away.

The brightly lit sign of the Hotel Polk flashes off and on. It illuminates the entire roof. But still Bolt doesn't notice you.

How can you get his attention?

Suddenly an idea zips through your mind. That's it! A sure way for Bolt to know you are on the hotel roof and desperately need his help.

You reach into your EMERGENCY KIT.

HOW DO YOU ATTRACT BOLT'S ATTENTION?

SOLUTION

You grab some marbles from your emergency kit. One at a time, you throw them at the letters O,T,O,L, and K. The letters smash and showers of glass cascade down on the roof.

Now the remaining letters on the lit-up sign spell H-E-L-P. These letters flash on and off.

XVI
The Hidden Headquarters

$\mathbf{B}$olt looks up at the hotel roof. He sees your signal.

Again you shout, "Bolt!" This time he sees you and waves. You wave back.

Bolt enters the Hotel Polk. He is coming to the rescue. You stand by the locked roof door, anxiously awaiting your partner.

Minutes seem like hours. Then you hear the door handle rattle. A voice calls from the other side. "I'm here, Ace!" Bolt shouts.

A lock clicks and the roof door swings open.

There, facing you, is Bolt. He has a grin on his face. "Let's get out of here fast!" he exclaims.

Back on the street, Bolt turns to you.

"Neat signal," he says. "At first I couldn't understand why those letters were going out one by one."

You both run down a side street. By the light of a full moon you make out Bolt's motorcycle parked against a building.

"Why don't we stop and rest a minute," you say to your friend.

"We can't stop just yet," answers Bolt. "We've got to reach Dr. XXX's headquarters while it's still dark."

"Where is Dr. XXX's headquarters?" you ask.

Bolt gives you a startled look. "I thought you knew," he says.

You shake your head.

Just then a long black car comes screeching around the corner. Bolt pulls you into the shadows.

"That car belongs to Dr. XXX," he says. "Let's follow it."

You put on your helmets and hop on the motorcycle. Then quickly you speed away.

You follow the car for several miles.

At Farmington Square the car stops. A man in a black jacket gets out and hurries down the street. The man turns onto a well-lit avenue lined with factory buildings.

Bolt stops the motorcycle and parks it.

"I'll follow him from across the street," says Bolt. "You stay on this side, farther behind. That way he is less likely to spot us."

Bolt begins walking slowly, cautiously following the man. He stays close to the walls of the factory buildings, out of the glare of streetlights. You follow on your side.

Suddenly the man stops and turns around. Bolt ducks into a doorway out of sight.

You hide in the shadows farther behind. Then the man continues down the street.

Soon he comes to a small park. The street is different now. It is lined with tall trees and neatly trimmed bushes.

Behind the trees you see a high wire fence. "Look," says Bolt, joining you. "That fence runs all around the block. We must be at Dr. XXX's hidden headquarters!"

You both stoop down behind a large bush. From your hiding place, you watch the man turn down a cobblestone path that leads into the park.

Suddenly dozens of spotlights turn on and shine directly at him. Now you can see a guard standing in front of a large iron gate. The man in the black jacket reaches into his pocket and pulls out a card. He hands it to the guard.

Then the guard walks over and heaves open the iron gate. The man enters the grounds and disappears in the distance.

The lights go off. It is dark again, except for a faint spray of moonlight.

"Ace," whispers your partner. "We've got to get over that fence."

You follow your partner as he circles the block.

Suddenly something runs across your path, and you jump! But it's only a cat — a black cat.

Where did the cat come from? You drop to your knees to examine the fence. Sure enough, there is a small hole in the bottom of the fence.

You whisper to your partner, "I think I can wiggle through the hole."

Bolt stoops down to check it. "I can't spread open the wires to make the hole any bigger," he says. "It's not large enough for me to slip through."

Rising slowly, Bolt firmly places his hand on your shoulder. "I guess it's up to you."

You gulp as your partner continues. "Good luck, Ace," he says. "You're on your own."

You wiggle through the hole to the other side of the wire fence. So far, so good, you think.

Ahead of you is a field with trees growing all around. In the far distance you see a large building. Lights shine brightly from its roof. That must be Dr. XXX's headquarters.

You feel tired and cold, but you reach into your EMERGENCY KIT for an Energy Bar and take a big bite. Soon you feel ready to move on.

You approach the headquarters and drop down into the tall grass. Then you silently crawl on your stomach toward the large building.

You get to a side door. At last you have reached your destination. But what should you do next? Is Dr. XXX inside?

Standing up, you press your ear to the door, listening intently for noises inside. But you don't hear a sound. It seems safe to enter.

Inch by inch, you push open the door. Beads of

perspiration dot your forehead. Finally, you shove it wide open and walk in.

Now you really are scared. Dr. XXX must be somewhere inside the building. But where?

Two doorways lead off the hall.

You stand flat against the wall and slowly shuffle sideways toward the first doorway.

As you peek inside, you can't believe what you see. The huge room has a high ceiling and a concrete floor. It looks cold and scary.

In the center stands a giant kettle, with smoke curling out of the top.

You tiptoe over to the kettle and notice letters are written on it. The letters say . . . SLUDGE!

A chill runs through you. This must be the room where Dr. XXX prepares his deadly poison.

What you see next gives you even more of a chill. Slumped in a chair at the far end of the room is a glassy-eyed figure. It's a guy about your age. He's mumbling something over and over again.

What is it? You strain to hear.

". . . I am a ZOMBIE . . . I am a ZOMBIE . . ."

It's Agent Cody!

But there's no time to help Agent Cody now, because a voice suddenly booms in the room.

"Stand where you are. Don't make a move or I'll shoot."

It's Dr. XXX! You've been discovered!

You stand there frozen and look up near the top of the wall across the room.

High above you is a large pipe. It stretches from one wall across to the other. A ladder leads up to the pipe.

You notice a window near one end of the pipe. Then you get an idea.

You quickly scamper up the ladder. Dropping on your stomach, you crawl along the pipe toward the window.

You look down at the floor below. It is a 30-foot drop. You wrap your arms and knees around the pipe, hugging it as tightly as you can. One slip and you will fall to the floor below.

A booming voice rings out.

"Now I've got you!"

You look down. There is Dr. XXX looking up directly at you. He lets out a loud, horrible laugh.

"You're trapped!" yells Dr. XXX. "That window can't be opened. I'm coming up to get you."

Your eyes widen as you see Dr. XXX heading for the ladder. He is coming after you!

You inch yourself further along the pipe, not knowing what else to do.

As Dr. XXX climbs up the ladder, your mind flashes through the things in your EMERGENCY KIT.

Then you have it! As Dr. XXX reaches the pipe, you carefully reach inside the kit.

WHAT CAN YOU USE TO STOP DR. XXX?

SOLUTION

You take out your two jelly sandwiches and open them.

Then you smear the gooey jelly all around the pipe behind you.

XVII
The Ape and You

You slowly inch toward the window as Dr. XXX crawls after you. But when he reaches the jelly, he slips and lets out a loud yell.

Dr. XXX tumbles downward, screaming as he falls.

You hug the pipe and look directly down at the floor beneath you.

Where is Dr. XXX? Then you see a string of bubbles emerge from the kettle of SLUDGE. The last one explodes with a large POP! Then all is silence.

Dr. XXX has landed in the cauldron of SLUDGE! That's the last you'll ever see of *him*.

Now is your chance to get to the ape!

Carefully, you turn around on the pipe. You hug on to it for dear life. Some of the slippery jelly still covers the spot where Dr. XXX fell, but you reach the ladder and breathe a sigh of relief. Then you slowly climb down, rung by rung.

Now where is the ape, you ask yourself?

Then you hear a strange sound. It seems to come from a room above you.

Quietly, you sneak up the stairs. And when you reach the top you freeze — in horror.

There, in the center of the hallway, stands a large cage. Inside is a huge ape, his hands gripping two bars and shaking them violently.

You take two steps toward the animal. It lets out an ear-splitting growl. Again you stop in your tracks.

Horner's instructions were perfectly clear. You are to deactivate the SLUDGE and erase the secret formula tattooed on the ape's head.

But how will you ever get to the ape?

Impossible!

You remember the items in your emergency kit. The sleeping potion will knock out the ape. But how will you ever get him to swallow it?

An idea flashes through your mind. Maybe the ape would like to share an Energy Bar.

Opening the kit, you take out the bar and wrap some string around it.

You grab a nearby broom and tie the other end of the string to it. Then you slowly creep toward the ape.

GROWL!

The ape can't hurt you, you think, so long as you don't get too close. You approach the cage carefully — very carefully — staying just far enough away.

GROWL!

Holding one end of the broom, you position it above the cage. The candy bar hangs down, just like a worm on a fishing pole.

Suddenly the growling has stopped. The ape looks up at the thing dangling above his head. He paws at the bar, and opens his mouth wide as if it will drop inside.

As the ape paws at the dangling Energy Bar, you think about the bottle of sleeping potion Horner gave you.

Can you climb on top of the cage and pour it into his open mouth?

Not a chance! The ape will grab your arm.

Your mind twists and turns, thinking of ways to outwit the animal. Then you think you have an answer — a way to slip the potion into the ape's mouth. And without getting too close.

Look inside your EMERGENCY KIT.

HOW CAN YOU PUT THE APE TO SLEEP?

SOLUTION

You remove a rubber glove from the kit. With the scissors, you cut a tiny hole in one of its fingers. Then you carefully pour the sleeping potion into the glove.

Tying the other end of the glove, you squeeze the liquid inside. The sleeping potion shoots out of the tiny hole in a long thin stream.

It's just like a squirt gun!

XVIII
The Secret Formula

With one hand you dangle the Energy Bar above the ape. He opens his mouth wide as you lower the candy bar.

In your other hand is the glove. Taking careful aim, you point it at the ape and squeeze. You squeeze and squeeze again.

Then you stand back and watch as the ape licks his lips.

GROWL!

This time his sound seems weaker.

G-r-o-w-l!

You stare in amazement as the ape slides down the bars and falls to the cage floor — asleep.

Now is your chance! You tiptoe over to the cage. The animal doesn't stir.

With the broom handle, you carefully tap the animal. Still no movement. The sleeping potion is working.

You quickly take the scissors, reach through the bars of the cage, and begin cutting the hair on the ape's head.

As the hair falls away, it reveals exactly what you have been looking for.

There on the head of the ape is tattooed the secret formula for SLUDGE!

You take out the ink remover from your kit and rub it on the animal's head. But the secret message won't disappear. The ink remover isn't strong enough. The formula is still there!

You scratch your head, frustrated that you have come so far but you still need to complete your final mission. The secret formula must be destroyed.

You think for a moment. Maybe the EMER-GENCY KIT can help. Then you realize it contains the answer to your problem.

WHAT DO YOU DO NEXT?

SOLUTION

You take out the pen, the one with the permanent black ink.

If the ink remover can't erase the formula, maybe you can scribble *over* it.

XIX
Mission Accomplished

You hastily scribble ink marks all over the formula, blacking it out completely.

There! The ape's forehead is completely black. No one can see through the ink to read the formula — now or ever.

You grab the Energy Bar and munch on it while admiring your work. Then you suddenly realize you have more work to do.

You rush down the steps and into the room with the SLUDGE. Opening the bottle of antidote, you pour it into the kettle.

The liquid inside bubbles with a thunderous noise. Just as suddenly, the noise stops. Now the SLUDGE is harmless!

Gripping the bottle with the remaining antidote, you hurry over to the dazed Cody.

"Drink!" you order.

The MUCK has an amazing effect. Immediately, Cody jumps up and starts doing a tap dance.

"There's no time for that now!" you mumble as you drag him toward the front door. Quickly you push it open with a big shove.

Pulling Cody behind you, you hurry along, taking in gulps of air as you try to catch your breath. Agent Cody seems to be coming to his senses. "Thanks for saving me, pal," he says solemnly.

"No problem," you tell him. As you near the hole in the fence, a feeling of relief sweeps over you.

You begin to realize what you have just done. You have saved the entire country, and the world, from Dr. XXX's evil plan!

Horner will be pleased. Bolt will be, too.

Now you're glad that he picked you for this dangerous assignment.

As you and Cody race for the fence, you mutter softly to yourself.

"Mission accomplished. Mission accomplished."

MISSION ACCOMPLISHED!